Mammoth Cave
National Park

by Mike Graf

Bridgestone Books
an imprint of Capstone Press
Mankato, Minnesota

Bridgestone Books are published by Capstone Press
151 Good Counsel Drive, P.O. Box 669, Mankato, Minnesota 56002
http://www.capstone-press.com

Library of Congress Cataloging-in-Publication Data
Graf, Mike.
    Mammoth Cave National Park/by Mike Graf.
    v.cm.—(National parks)
    Includes bibliographical references (p. 23) and index.
    "Internet sites": p. 24
    Contents: Mammoth Cave National Park—How Mammoth Cave formed—People
at Mammoth Cave—Animals—Plants—Weather—Activities—Safety—Park issues—Map
activity—About national parks—Words to know.
    ISBN 0-7368-2221-6
    1. Mammoth Cave National Park (Ky.)—Juvenile literature. [1. Mammoth Cave
National Park (Ky.) 2. National parks and reserves.] I. Title. II. Series: Graf, Mike.
National parks.
F457 .M2G73 2004
551.44'7'09769754—dc21   2002154711

Editorial Credits
Heather Adamson, editor; Linda Clavel, series designer; Enoch Peterson, book designer;
    Anne McMullen, illustrator; Alta Schaffer, photo researcher; Karen Risch, product
    planning editor

Photo Credits
Aurora/Stephen Alvarez, 4, 16
Corbis/David Muench, cover
Finley-Holiday Film Corp., 10
Kent and Donna Dannen, 6, 14
Library of Congress, 8 (all)
Mammoth Cave National Park Service, 1, 18, 19
Visuals Unlimited/Rob & Ann Simpson, 12; R. Knolan Benfield, Jr., 17

Special thanks to the National Park Service for reviewing this text for accuracy.

1 2 3 4 5 6 08 07 06 05 04 03

Table of Contents

Mammoth Cave National Park 5

How Mammoth Cave Formed 7

People in Mammoth Cave 9

Animals 11

Plants 13

Weather. 15

Activities 16

Safety 17

Park Issues 18

Map Activity 20

About National Parks 22

Words to Know 23

Read More 23

Useful Addresses. 24

Internet Sites 24

Index 24

Kentucky

Mammoth Cave National Park

Mammoth Cave is the world's longest cave. It has more than 360 miles (580 kilometers) of mapped cave passages. Mammoth Cave is three times longer than any known cave in the world.

Mammoth Cave National Park covers 53,000 acres (21,000 hectares) in Kentucky. About 1.7 million people visit the park every year.

The area above and around Mammoth Cave is filled with forests, springs, and sinkholes. The ground falls in where sinkholes form. The huge cave is underneath these sinkholes.

In 1941, the U.S. government made the area of Mammoth Cave a national park. The government creates national parks to protect special natural areas. People cannot build or hunt on park lands. But they can camp, hike, and view the wildlife and scenery in the park.

Mammoth Cave National Park contains Mammoth Cave, the world's longest cave.

6

How Mammoth Cave Formed

Millions of years ago, a shallow sea covered the Mammoth Cave area. Tiny animals that lived in the sea left behind skeletons. Over time, the skeletons formed a layer of limestone.

After the sea dried up, a river dumped sand on the limestone. The sand became sandstone. Over time, the limestone and sandstone layers started to crack.

Rain and riverwater mixed with chemicals in the air and soil. This mixture formed acid. The acid leaked into the cracks. Over many years, acid broke down the limestone underground. This process created a series of caves.

Dripping water helped cave formations develop. Many strange and beautiful cave formations are found within Mammoth Cave. Stalactite formations hang from the cave's ceiling. Stalagmites rise from the ground.

Cave formations, such as stalactites and columns, form over time from dripping water.

People in Mammoth Cave

People have been in the Mammoth Cave area for more than 10,000 years. American Indians hunted along area rivers. Later, they explored parts of the cave and used some of its minerals.

European settlers discovered the cave in the late 1700s. They mined saltpeter from the cave. They used this mineral to make gunpowder. In the 1800s, slaves worked in the saltpeter mines.

In 1816, people started to tour Mammoth Cave. Stephen Bishop and Mat and Nick Bransford were slaves who guided visitors through the cave. Relatives of Bishop and the Bransfords led cave tours for more than 100 years.

In 1925, cave explorer Floyd Collins became trapped in a cave near Mammoth Cave. The world followed the story to learn if rescuers would save him. Collins died before rescuers could get him out. This event brought attention to all the caves in the area, including Mammoth Cave.

People began touring Mammoth Cave in the 1800s. Stephen Bishop (bottom) guided many of the first tours.

10

Animals

Mammoth Cave is famous for its cave wildlife. Many different kinds of animals make use of the cave. Some animals such as crickets and bats spend only part of the day in the cave.

Troglobites are animals that spend their whole lives in a cave. Their bodies have adapted to caves so they cannot live anywhere else. Mammoth Cave's troglobites include eyeless fish and crayfish.

Salamanders, springfish, and spiders live in cool, dark places. Mammoth Cave makes a good home for these animals. It is always cool and dark in the cave.

The hilly, wooded area above and around Mammoth Cave is also home to wildlife. Visitors often see deer, wild turkeys, squirrels, chipmunks, and raccoons roaming the woods. Coyotes, bobcats, foxes, minks, and weasels hunt in the area. Ducks, kingfishers, and blue herons live near rivers. The park also has many types of fish, turtles, and snakes.

Eyeless fish are one of the troglobite animals that have adapted to Mammoth Cave.

Plants

Mammoth Cave National Park is filled with plant life. Forests cover the ground above and around the cave. Sycamore trees grow along the banks of rivers. Tulip, poplar, sugar maple, and beech trees live in moist areas. Oak trees cover drier areas of the park.

One small part of the park contains an old-growth forest. Trees in this area were never cut down before Mammoth Cave became a park. This forest preserves trees that once grew all over the hills of Kentucky.

Many different plants grow throughout the park. Rangers have counted 872 types of flowering plants in the park. Phlox, violets, and trilliums are common wildflowers. Rangers also protect the 21 kinds of plants that are in danger of disappearing from the park.

Many kinds of trees and plants grow in the area above and around Mammoth Cave.

14

Weather

No matter what the weather is like outside the cave, it is always 54 degrees Fahrenheit (12 degrees Celsius) inside Mammoth Cave. The weather outside does not affect the cave at all.

Above ground, spring weather varies the most. It can be 30 degrees Fahrenheit (minus 1 degree Celsius) one day. Other days it may be 80 degrees Fahrenheit (27 degrees Celsius). Spring also brings rains showers and sometimes snow.

Summer is the warmest and wettest season. Temperatures can rise to 100 degrees Fahrenheit (38 degrees Celsius). Thunderstorms happen often in the summer.

Fall has good hiking weather. It is sunny but cool. It does not rain often, and it rarely snows.

Winter is usually cold, wet, and foggy. Most of the park's snowfall occurs in January and February. Temperatures can drop far below freezing during the winter.

The leaves on many of the park's trees begin to turn color in early fall.

Activities

Most people come to the park to tour Mammoth Cave. Some tours take visitors to the most interesting cave formations. One tour takes visitors into the cave using lanterns. The "Trog Tour" is just for children. Kids crawl, slither, and climb through narrow cave openings.

Visitors to Mammoth Cave also enjoy camping, hiking, mountain biking, canoeing, fishing, and rock climbing.

Safety

People touring the cave need to be careful. Some paths have uneven ground or many steps to climb. Other cave trails pass steep drop-offs. Cave trails may be wet or slippery. Visitors need to wear hiking shoes and follow tour instructions.

The timber rattlesnake and the northern copperhead are poisonous snakes that live within the park boundaries. While hiking, visitors should watch where they put their hands and feet. Visitors should also know how to identify these snakes.

Rangers at Mammoth Cave are concerned about air pollution. A coal-burning power plant is being built near the park. The power plant will make the air pollution even worse. Air pollution can kill plants and animals.

Overgrown plants called "wildland fuels" are burned on purpose at the park. This activity helps prevent larger wildfires from happening later.

Park workers sometimes set fires to prevent larger wildfires from happening.

Rangers are also working to help return natural plants to the park. They remove plants that settlers brought to the area and restore the original plants.

Water pollution is another park issue. Rivers and streams flow into the park. Polluted water could get into the cave. This would ruin the cave's environment. Life in the cave could be destroyed.

Rangers and park workers plant trees and plants that are natural to the area.

Map Activity

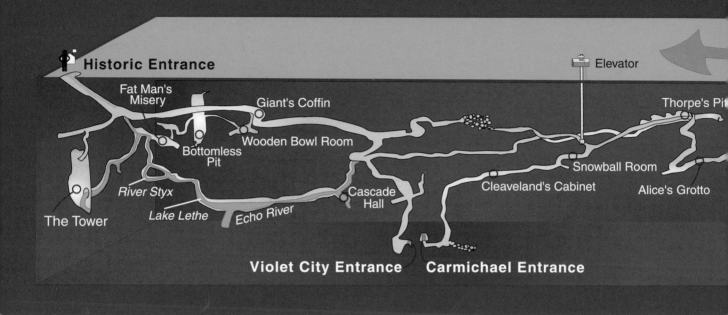

Mammoth Cave National Park has many paths that wind by the cave's famous formations. Giant's Coffin, The Tower, Bottomless Pit, Grand Canyon, Moonlight Dome, Frozen Niagara, and the Snowball Room are a few. See how far it is from one formation to another formation.

What You Need
20-inch (51-centimeter) piece of string

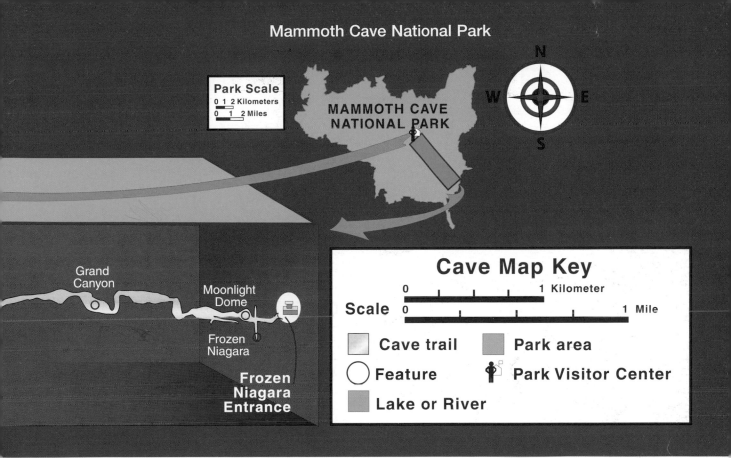

Mammoth Cave National Park

Park Scale

0 1 2 Kilometers

0 1 2 Miles

MAMMOTH CAVE
NATIONAL PARK

N
W E
S

Grand
Canyon

Moonlight
Dome

Frozen
Niagara

Frozen
Niagara
Entrance

Cave Map Key

Scale

0   1 Kilometer

0   1 Mile

Cave trail   Park area

Feature   Park Visitor Center

Lake or River

What You Do

1. Find the cave trails on the map. Pick one of the cave's entrances as a starting place. Then, choose a cave feature as your destination.
2. Measure the distance you have to walk. Place one end of the string on the trail at your selected entrance. Then lay the string down following the winding path of the trail until you reach your feature.
3. Use the scale to measure the length of string and find the distance in miles or kilometers. Try this with several other places in the cave.

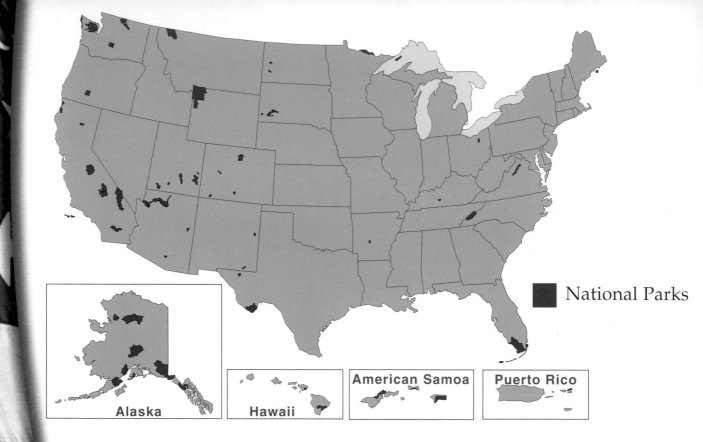

National Parks

Alaska

Hawaii

American Samoa

Puerto Rico

About National Parks

In 1916, the U.S. government formed the National Park Service. This organization was created to oversee all national park lands. Today, the United States has more than 50 national parks. The National Park Service also oversees nearly 400 other areas. These sites include recreational areas, natural landmarks, and historic sites such as battlefields.

Words to Know

environment (en-VYE-ruhn-muhnt)—the natural world of land, water, and air

pollution (puh-LOO-shuhn)—materials that hurt Earth's water, air, and land

saltpeter (SAWLT-pee-tur)—a mineral used to make gunpowder; saltpeter used to be mined from Mammoth Cave.

sinkhole (SINGK-hohl)—a low area or dip in the ground caused by a cave or collapsed area underground

stalactite (stuh-LAK-tite)—a rock formation that hangs from the ceiling of a cave

stalagmite (stuh-LAG-mite)—a rock formation that rises from the floor of a cave

troglobite (TRAWG-loh-bite)—an animal that can only survive in a cave environment

Read More

Burnham, Brad. *Mammoth Cave: The World's Longest Cave System.* Famous Caves of the World. New York: PowerKids Press, 2003.

Oliver, Clare. *Life in a Cave.* Microhabitats. Austin, Texas: Raintree Steck-Vaughn, 2002.

Raatma, Lucia. *Our National Parks.* Let's See. Minneapolis: Compass Point Books, 2002.

Useful Addresses

Mammoth Cave National Park
P.O. Box 7
Mammoth Cave, KY
42259-0007

National Park Service
1849 C Street NW
Washington, DC 20240

Internet Sites

Do you want to find out more about Mammoth Cave National Park? Let FactHound, our fact-finding hound dog, do the research for you.

Here's how:
1) Visit *http://www.facthound.com*
2) Type in the **Book ID** number: **0736822216**
3) Click on **FETCH IT**.

FactHound will fetch Internet sites picked by our editors just for you!

Index

animals, 7, 11, 17, 18
Bishop, Stephen, 9
Collins, Floyd, 9
Kentucky, 5, 13
limestone, 7
plant life, 13, 18, 19
pollution, 18, 19

saltpeter, 9
sinkhole, 5
stalactite, 7
stalagmite, 7
troglobites, 11
Trog Tour, 16
weather, 15